Sidney Crosby

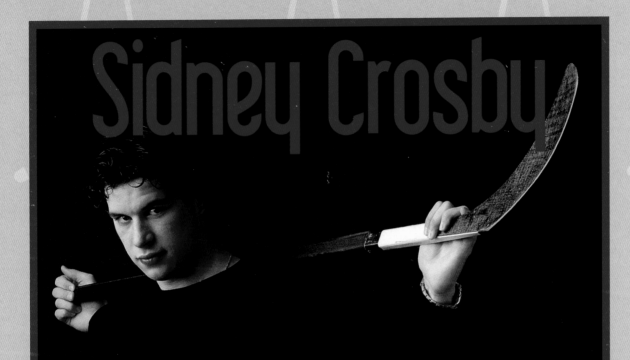

Danielle LeClair

Weigl

Published by Weigl Educational Publishers Limited
6325 10th Street S.E.
Calgary, Alberta T2H 2Z9
Website: www.weigl.com

Library and Archives Canada Cataloguing-in-Publication Data available upon request.
Fax 1-866-44-WEIGL for the attention of the Publishing Records department.

ISBN 978-1-77071-596-7 (hard cover)
ISBN 978-1-77071-602-5 (soft cover)

Printed in the United States of America in North Mankato, Minnesota
1 2 3 4 5 6 7 8 9 0 14 13 12 11 10

072010
WEP230610

Editor: Aaron Carr   **Design**: Kenzie Browne

All of the Internet URLs given in the book were valid at the time of publication. However, due to the dynamic nature of the Internet, some addresses may have changed, or sites may have ceased to exist since publication. While the author and publisher regret any inconvenience this may cause readers, no responsibility for any such changes can be accepted by either the author or the publisher.

Weigl gratefully acknowledges the financial support of the Government of Canada through the Canada Book Fund for our publishing activities.

Photo Credits
Weigl acknowledges Getty Images as its primary image supplier for this title.

Every reasonable effort has been made to trace ownership and to obtain permission to reprint copyright material. The publishers would be pleased to have any errors or omissions brought to their attention so that they may be corrected in subsequent printings.

CONTENTS

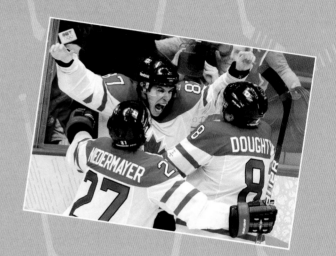

Who is Sidney Crosby?

Sidney Crosby is a professional hockey player. He is one of the best players in the National Hockey League (NHL).

Crosby loved to play hockey while growing up. Soon, people noticed his skills on the ice. As Crosby got older, people compared him to well-known Canadian hockey player Wayne Gretzky.

Gretzky is called "The Great One." Many people call Crosby "The Next One."

Growing Up

Sidney Patrick Crosby was born on August 7, 1987, in Cole Harbour, Nova Scotia. Crosby's father, Troy, was a hockey player. The Montreal Canadiens **drafted** Troy in 1984, but he never played with the team.

Troy later took a job doing maintenance work at a law firm. Crosby's mother, Trina, worked at a grocery store.

With his father coaching him, Crosby soon became known as a skilled hockey player. By the time he was seven years old, Crosby was giving interviews to local sports reporters.

Nova Scotia, Home of Sidney Crosby

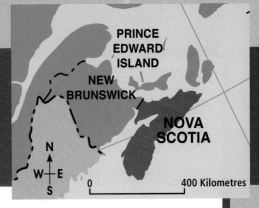

PRINCE EDWARD ISLAND
NEW BRUNSWICK
NOVA SCOTIA

N W E S

0   400 Kilometres

- Crosby's name appears on the sign welcoming people to his hometown of Cole Harbour.
- Like Crosby, hockey legend Al MacInnis is from Nova Scotia. MacInnis is the third-highest scoring NHL defenceman of all time.
- NHL players Joe DePenta, Cam Russell, and Craig Hillier all come from Cole Harbour.
- When Crosby won the Stanley Cup in 2009, about 25,000 people came to Cole Harbour to see the cup.

7

Overcoming Obstacles

Crosby's family did not have a great deal of money. His mother took a second job handing out flyers to help pay for Crosby to play hockey. Crosby earned money by working a paper route every Saturday.

Sometimes, being the best player on the team was a challenge for Crosby. Many teams would ignore the puck and chase him. Players on the other team would hit Crosby more than any other player on his team. They wanted to stop Crosby from scoring goals.

When Crosby was 14 and playing with 17-year-olds, he scored 217 points in one season.

Practice Makes Perfect

When Crosby was two years old, his father painted the basement floor to look like a hockey rink. Crosby used a hockey stick that was cut short to shoot pucks at the clothes dryer. At the age of three, Crosby got his first pair of ice skates. He joined a hockey league two years later.

When Crosby was 14 years old, he started working out every day with a **personal trainer**. That year, he led his team to a national championship. A year later, Crosby left home to play hockey at Shattuck-St. Mary's School in Minnesota. There, he scored 162 points in 57 games. Later, Crosby and his team played in the U.S. National championship.

Key Events

In 2003, Crosby became the first player in Quebec Major Junior Hockey League (QMJHL) history to win all of the league's top awards. He won player of the year, top **rookie**, and top scorer.

In 2004, Crosby was asked to play for Canada at the World Junior Hockey Championship. At 16, he was the youngest player on the team. Crosby is the youngest player ever to score for Canada.

When Crosby was 17 years old, he was one of the most highly valued draft picks in hockey history. The 2005 NHL draft **lottery** became known as the "Sidney Crosby Sweepstakes." The Pittsburgh Penguins won the draft lottery.

In his first NHL season, Crosby scored 102 points. This made him the youngest player in NHL history to score at least 100 points in a season. Crosby also broke the Penguins' team records for most assists and most points in a season by a rookie.

Influences

Crosby's family is the main influence in his life. When he was young, Crosby's parents went to all of his hockey games. Crosby's younger sister, Taylor, also plays hockey. He talks to Taylor about hockey when they are together.

Another influence in Crosby's life is former hockey player Mario Lemieux. Crosby started his NHL career with the Pittsburgh Penguins in 2005. Lemieux was the **captain** of the Penguins at the time.

For five years, Crosby lived with Lemieux and his family during the hockey season.

Achievements and Successes

Crosby has had many achievements in sports, as a role model, and in **charity** work. He has been the **most valuable player** (MVP) and top scorer in four different hockey leagues, including the NHL. In 2007, Crosby became the youngest captain in NHL history. He was 19 years and nine months old.

Crosby's success in hockey allows him to help others. Every year, Crosby donates Penguins tickets to families and children that cannot afford to buy their own tickets. Crosby also donates special seats to people who cannot sit in regular seats.

Crosby is the youngest player in NHL history to score 200 career points.

In 2007, Crosby won NHL awards for MVP, top scorer, and most outstanding player.

Two years later, Crosby became the youngest captain in NHL history to win a Stanley Cup. He led all playoff scorers, with 15 goals in 24 games.

On February 28, 2010, Crosby scored the game-winning goal in overtime of the Olympic gold medal game. He scored seven points in seven games during the Olympics.

What is a Hockey Player?

A hockey player is an athlete who plays on a hockey team. Hockey is played on ice with two teams. Each player wears skates. Both teams need at least six players on the ice at the same time. There is one goalie, three **forwards**, and two **defensive players**.

Each player moves the puck around the ice with a stick. Players try to shoot the puck into the other team's net. Goalies try to keep the puck out of the net.

Hockey Players Through History

Like Crosby, these hockey players have achieved success in the sport.

Mario Lemieux

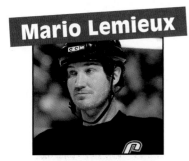

Lemieux is thought to be one of the greatest hockey players of all time. He led the Pittsburgh Penguins to two Stanley Cups. Lemieux also helped Canada win an Olympic gold medal and two World Cups of Hockey.

Wayne Gretzky

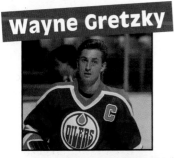

Gretzky scored more points than any other player in NHL history. He won NHL MVP nine times. Gretzky helped the Edmonton Oilers win the Stanley Cup four times. He is also the only NHL player to score 200 or more points in one season.

Cassie Campbell

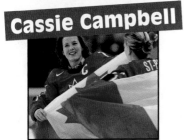

Campbell was the captain of the Canadian Women's hockey team at the 2002 and 2006 Winter Olympics. Her team won gold medals both years. She is the only hockey player to lead Canada to two Olympic gold medals.

Timeline

1987 Sidney Crosby is born on August 7 in Cole Harbour, Nova Scotia.

1990 Crosby gets his first pair of ice skates.

1994 The CBC television show *Hockey Day in Canada* airs a feature on Crosby.

2003 Crosby is drafted to the QMJHL team, the Rimouski Océanic.

2003	The Canadian Junior Hockey team wins the gold medal. Crosby scores in the championship game.
2005	The Pittsburgh Penguins pick Crosby first overall in the NHL entry draft.
2007	The Penguins name Crosby captain. This makes him the youngest captain in NHL history.
2009	Crosby becomes the youngest captain in NHL history to win the Stanley Cup.
2010	Crosby's overtime goal wins the Olympic gold medal for Team Canada. Canada beats the United States 3 to 2.

Write a Biography

A person's life story can be the subject of a book. This kind of book is called a biography. Biographies describe the lives of people who have had great success or done important things to help others. These people may be alive today, or they may have lived many years ago.

Try writing your own biography. First, decide who you want to write about. You can choose a hockey player, such as Sidney Crosby, or any other person you find interesting.

Then, find out if your library has any books about this person. Write down the key events in this person's life.

- What was this person's childhood like?
- What has he or she accomplished?
- What are his or her goals?
- What makes this person special or unusual?

Answer the questions in your notebook. Your answers will help you write a biography.

Find Out More

To learn more about Sidney Crosby, visit these websites.

Learn about Sidney Crosby at this site.
www.sidney-crosby.info

Discover facts about hockey and its history at this site.
www.nhl.com

Learn about other great hockey players at this site.
www.legendsofhockey.net/html/search.htm

Follow Crosby and his Pittsburgh Penguins teammates at this site.
http://penguins.nhl.com

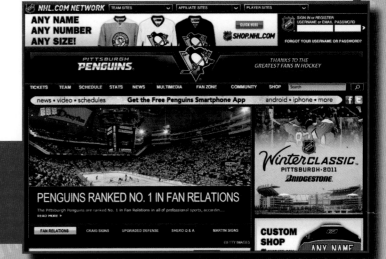

Glossary

captain: the player chosen to be the team leader by coaches and other players on the team

charity: giving help to those in need

defensive players: hockey players who focus on stopping the other teams from scoring

drafted: chosen to play for an NHL team at a yearly meeting

forwards: offensive players on a hockey team

lottery: a random draw; in NHL, used to determine the order teams must follow when choosing players

most valuable player: the player judged to be the best in the league by coaches and other players

personal trainer: a person who works with athletes to improve their strength, speed, balance, and endurance

rookie: an athlete in his or her first year of play in a league

Index